Poems 1/3

Michael Boy works as a writer and conceptual artist. He explores the feelings and peculiarities of special people and tries to capture moments through poetry. An approach and a confrontation.

These poems are dedicated to
Birgit, Max and Leo.

Bibliografische Information der
Deutschen Nationalbibliothek: Die
Deutsche Nationalbibliothek
verzeichnet diese Publikation in der
Deutschen Nationalbibliografie;
detaillierte bibliografische Daten sind
im Internet über dnb.dnb.de abrufbar.

Herstellung und Verlag:
BoD – Books on Demand,
Norderstedt

ISBN: 9783753471976

96 crazy short poems from the main volume "Poems".

Incomprehensible poems by and about special people. In search of encounters, self-discovery and self-help as a mixture of words. An affair of the heart.

Part 1

Often you've seen some things from
the front, and then you've seen some
things from the back. Everything is one
and the same. What is important is the
tender happiness and the quiet joy
within you. What do you think?

1. Wound

Do not treat the wound of the heart,
do not nourish the wound properly,
and do not leave everything in the
heart.

2. Alas

Unfortunately,
suffering does not always have a great
purpose,
but suffering always makes sense.

3. Trust

Gain confidence in your thoughts
and turn them into a big picture.

4.   Exchange
Exchange fluids,
thoughts and feelings
and solid knowledge,
faith and perseverance and yourself.

5.   Hopped off
Over and over
and then run away or not.

6.   Short
Facing the sun,
of course,
short and friendly,
although it hurts,
praise the sun,
short and very friendly.

7. Network
Insulting thinkers for explanations,
finding the right meaning.

8. Brutal
Drinking the last sip
and being cruel
without mercy is always a good trait.

9. Promise
Promise nothing
and be the center of the earth despite
the herd consciousness,
come here and surrender.

10. Warning
Gradually the memories disappear,
the accuser is old and thin,
it seems he is exhausted.

11. Reason
There is no real reason
for the accumulation of a large amount
of knowledge.

12. So that
Quite beside me,
definitely want to be there and keep in
touch.

A brief thought occurs to me in between, have I become funnier or more thoughtful as a result of the poems? The people about whom I write and from whom I have received many thoughts fascinate me and captivate me. Stubborn eccentrics without a fixed abode in the spirit.

13. Happiness
Good luck and control
over the worlds,
good luck.

14. Order
Get the order,
execute it well
and be proud of the warrior,
you must be a warrior.

15. Appearance
I came and learned everything,
an exemplary strong guy.

16. Miracles

No additional miracles happen,
what is known should be enough.

17. Frame

The frame has a beautiful frame
function,
which creates hope.

18. See

I couldn't see the sun for happiness
and looked forward to silliness.

19. Slowly
Come to yourself
and be a decent person,
strengthen your arms
and play with your muscles with joy.

20. Twisted
Think,
nod and confirm,
to confirm and think about the future,
be successful.

21. Weekend
Weekends,
end of year and end of life,
find everything effortlessly.

22. Noise
The constant noise in the small head
has become music,
sound and sound,
friendly to all,
be friendly.

23. Pay
If you pay for everything,
bills will not remain unpaid,
gifts are dangerous
and happiness will be a punishment.

24. Abbreviation
Since the shortcut has taken hold,
there is no longer any way to see
burdensome life in the long run.

25. Loaded

Well calculated,
smart, well calculated,
but at the same time clean
and yet a new beginning.

26. Words

There will always be words,
words that describe all life.

27. Delivered

Open rest,
the rest comes back
and everything else is near,
takes almost no space,
everything is open.

28. Finished
Get done,
get the job done
and have fun thinking every day
without thinking.

29. Vanity
Take your vanity
and lose yourself,
fall down.

30. Lights
And it shines the head,
many believe
that they may be infected.

31. Love
Here we should not forget love,
love for each other,
thoughtful love and empty love.

32. Replacement
Replace flowing things,
thoughts and thoughts,
feelings and hard knowledge,
belief and withdrawal,
and yourself.

33. Escape
Escape again and again
and again and again
and again and again
and again.

I have always loved reading poetry,
preferably lying under a tree
somewhere, drinking a delicious wine
or a good beer. I still love to read
poetry. I would be happy if you like
these poems here and enjoy them. My
inspirational friends would be happy
about that too.

34. Short

Of course the sun shines briefly and
kindly,
it hurts,
but the sun is admired
and briefly and so beautifully.

35. Network

Fertilize
the thinkers with an explanation
while searching for the right meaning.

36. Brutal

To drink the last cup
and be brutal is the character of a
timeless good character.

37. Promise
Don't promise anything,
come here
and surrender to the center of the earth
despite the swarming consciousness.

38. Warning
Slowly disappear the memory of life,
life is old and thin,
just be weak and stay weak.

39. Reason
There is no real reason
to accumulate much knowledge.

40. Like this
I
definitely want to be
alone.

41. Happiness
Do your best
to rule the world
happily.

42. Orders
Take orders,
carry them out properly
and be proud of the warrior,
you are a warrior.

43. Doer
I
have done
everything.

44. Miracle
There is no additional miracle,
the known should be
enough.

45. Frame
The frame has the beautiful framing
that the frame wants.

46. Happiness
I was happy,
couldn't see the sun
and was looking forward to silliness.

47. Slowly
Come back to your senses,
become a decent person,
strengthen your arms
and let views play for pleasure.

48. Imagination
If you think a lot to stimulate your
imagination,
be sure to look ahead
and improve yourself.

49. Weekend
Find everything on the weekend,
New Year,
without effort.

50. Noise
The constant sound in the small head is
music,
sound,
sound and good for everyone.

51. Number
Pay everything,
do not leave bills unpaid,
gifts are dangerous,
happiness is a heavy penalty.

52. Abbreviations
Shortcuts are so common that in the
long run
there is no shortcut to find a way out.

53. Number
It is well calculated,
intelligent,
well calculated
and still shaded,
but it is still a new beginning.

54. Words
There will always
be the word life.

55. Rest

The rest is open,
the rest is back,
everything else is everywhere,
needs some space
and everything is open.

56. Completed

Prepare now,
have the pleasure of thinking every day
without thinking too much.

57. Vanity

Seize vanity,
lose your sight
and fall.

58. Light
And it comes to light,
and many believe
that they can be infected.

59. Eclipse
Have seen the plan
and think the day well,
sentences invert the world,
just come through it
and be there.

60. Wrung out
Well wrung out the construct,
catch the good inventions of life.

Today I was with my son in the city and ate an ice cream with him. That was really good. The togetherness. The ice cream and the hustle and bustle in the city. My son is autistic and can rarely wait. When I stand in the long line to buy the ice cream, he waits patiently. This is a great exception. Waiting can be nice.

61. Games
Reinvent old games,
feel briefly secure
and talk to yourself.

62. Rain
The raindrop sticks to the glass,
the thoughts stick to life with the
raindrop
and meet you.

63. Illusion
The illusion of knowledge narrows my
good work breaks
and I breathe.

64. Attitude
Fine sounds emerge from the noises
and the attitude gets an additional
narrowing
and the morning sun warms.

65. Reason
A very good reason to live
is to know better without being caught,
by oneself or by others.

66. Nose
Orientation by the nose
helps to get to the destination
and to die.

67. Watch out
The smell on the fingers
opens a new world
and captures.

68. Without
Especially the word without has great
content
and likes to take us
to the beginning into an innocent
world
and turns us around.

69. Useful
Useful is good to us
and must not be lost until the end.

70. Finite

Finite takes us into an infinity,
let us examine opinions,
gladly we just adopt them.

71. Condition

The good condition of the neglected
shocks
and makes us think,
because performance counts
and then I may.

72. Sun

Innocently
the sun penetrates the sunburn.

73. Blooming
Briefly the old man blossoms,
looks into the merry circle
and takes the last train home,
all seems well.

74. Desolate
The fish is already stinking
and the hungry
are impatiently scolding you.

75. Buds
Excited,
everyone runs blindly to their doom,
breathing short and aging fast.

76. Leg-hard
Currently you must be leg-hard
and endure much torment,
so you can go to heaven
and finally be happy.

77. Initially
The train left in the beginning,
no one heard a sound,
it hasn't been so quiet for ages
and again in the beginning.

78. Unfounded
To have forgotten everything
and to be accused unfoundedly
friendly.

79. Gear
Travelling long distances
and arriving at the thoughts of others,
breaking up and dividing
and sliding away.

80. Sense
In turning around
lies buried a great mystery
and remains unknown.

81. Hand
Squeeze the enemy's hand without
strength
and give up life and happiness suddenly
comes flying and create.

82. Glass

The breaking glass remained in the
mind,
no one expected the end now.

83. Food

Quickly gulp down the food
and be an epicure,
more makes the right to be an epicure
and distinguishes.

84. Liberation

Out of weariness go to church
and with the scratching thoughts hope
for the final liberation,
well done.

85. Again

Again and again
the good righteous appear disgustingly
unrighteous.

86. Alien

Not being at home in the garden,
hoping in the extraterrestrial the
explanation for today,
taking all mysticism in the plastic bag.

87. Punctual

Wearing the right shirt at the right time
and getting to the funeral on time.

88. Dreamy
Fly dreamily through the air,
breathe in the scent of other people,
wash myself
and be a dreamer of the best kind.

89. Heroes
Since I got a medal,
I can now call myself
a human being.

90. High
The clouds in the sky seem to fly quite
high,
know by heart the past,
be a decal and laugh.

Many poems in this book are inspired by people with autism and by people who have no ordinary consciousness, or are simply mentally always somewhere else, not here in our commonly imagined world. At least that's how one imagines it. Is there an ordinary, common world?

91. Any
For good reasons,
the driver could not stop,
any responsibility was on the others,
and love was also a word.

92. Quickly
The bird on the window
sill chirps my morning song way too
fast.

93. Out
How far still go out to be high,
play with life and become more
and be higher,
have done well.

94. Responsibility
I'll give you the responsibility,
it's really none of my business,
just like you.

95. Worm
The worm
has found your hole of thoughts
and finds a home here
and stays with you
for the rest of your life.

96. Heart
With an empty heart I meet my heart,
with an empty heart I meet your heart,
with an empty heart I meet being.